OX-CART MAN

by
Donald Hall

Teacher Guide

Written by
Jean Jamieson

Note
The Puffin Books paperback edition of the book was used to prepare this teacher guide. The page references may differ in the hardcover or other paperback editions.

ISBN 1-56137-457-1

Printed in the United States of America.

To order, contact your local school supply store, or—

Novel Units, Inc.
P.O. Box 97
Bulverde, TX 78163-0097

Web site: www.educyberstor.com

Table of Contents

Skills and Strategies

Comprehension
Predicting, sequencing

Literary Elements
Characterization, story elements

Writing
Narrative

Thinking
Brainstorming

Vocabulary
Alphabetical order

Listening/Speaking
Discussion

Summary of *Ox-Cart Man*

This story describes the day-to-day life of an early nineteenth century New England farm family throughout the changing seasons. As winter approaches, the father of the family takes the goods to market that the family members have been working on throughout the year. He returns with something special for each, and the process starts anew.

About the Author

Donald Hall was born September 29, 1928, in New Haven, Connecticut. He attended Philips Exeter Academy, 1944-47; Harvard University, B.A. 1951; Oxford University, B. Lit., 1953; attended Stanford University, 1953-54. He has been a professor, an editorial consultant for a publisher, an editor of books, an author of poetry books, plays, and an author of books for children and textbooks for adults.
Hall started to write poetry at the age of fourteen. Although he acts occasionally, he stays with the lecture circuit, an indulgence he is naturally quite fond of, for it allows him to play the role of the poet and actor at the same time.

On the writing of prose, Hall has given this advice: "A writer must become honest in the expression of himself, which means that he must know himself. It means learning the real names of feelings."
With regard to the story of *Ox-Cart Man*, he has said: "I heard the story from my cousin Paul Fenton, my grandfather's nephew. Paul told me he had heard it when he was a boy from an old man who told him that he had heard it when he was a boy, from an old man who told him that he had heard it when he was a boy, from an old man. It is always told as a true story, and I believe it. I was thrilled with it, thinking of man's past life described in cyclical fashion, dying in order to be born again, as if human beings could be perennial plants." Hall wrote *Ox-Cart Man* first as a poem for the *New Yorker*.

About the Illustrator

Barbara Cooney was born August 6, 1917, in Brooklyn, New York. Her childhood was spent on Long Island where she attended Great Neck Preparatory School. She also attended Briarcliff School; Smith College; and the Art Students League, New York.
Barbara Cooney says of her childhood, "My mother painted pictures for fun, so her children did, too. That's how it all began."

A leaflet published about her by the University of Southern Mississippi states: "Ideas for her books just happen; some texts take reworking. But she works on her pictures until they are as perfect as she can get them. Her work, which includes photography, is interrelated with her life. Her books are gay, entertaining and true to life as she sees it. Is it any wonder that children young and old enjoy books by Barbara Cooney?"

In 1975, the University of Southern Mississippi presented her with their Children's Collection Medallion for outstanding contributions in the field of children's books. She also received the Smith College Medal in 1976. She received the Caldecott Medal in 1958 for *Chanticleer and the Fox*, and in 1980 for *Ox-Cart Man.*

The Caldecott Medal

The Caldecott Medal, named for Randolph Caldecott, is awarded annually by the American Library Association to the illustrator of the most distinguished American picture book for children. Randolph Caldecott, an English illustrator, was born in Chester, England, March 22, 1846. He died in St. Augustine, Florida, February 12, 1886. He had a great talent, and loved horses, dogs, and everything that belonged to the English countryside. His drawings were noted for their freshness, boldness, and gaiety. He thought long and seriously before putting pen to paper. He said, "The fewer the lines, the less error committed!"

Although Caldecott and his wife never had children of their own, he had many children as friends. It was for children that he did the work for which he will probably be longest remembered and best loved.

Introductory Activities

Initiating Activity

The Cart: These are some of the things that the Ox-Cart Man took to Portsmouth to sell: wool, shawl, mittens, candles, birch brooms, potatoes, apples, honey, honeycombs, turnips, cabbages, maple sugar, goose feathers, linen. Collect as many of the items as you can before starting this activity. When ready to begin, place the items around the room, hanging some mobile-style.

After the children gather in a group, draw their attention to the cart on the bulletin board. Ask them if they know what that is, what it is used for, discuss its use at present, if any. How are goods taken from place to place to be sold at the present time? Can anyone think of when something like the cart would have been used? Who might have used it?

Teach the children the song that follows, and discuss with them things that could be put into the cart and taken somewhere to be sold, as the blanks are filled in. (Sung to the tune of "She'll Be Comin' Round The Mountain." See Bibliography, Beall-Sing-alongs.)

Oh, I have some things in the cart to sell,
Oh, I have some things in the cart to sell.
They are piled to the top,
Just tell me when to stop.
Oh, I have some things in the cart to sell.
I have ______________ and ___________ to sell.
I have ______________ and ___________ to sell.
You will like what you see.
Won't you buy something from me?
Oh, I have some things in the cart to sell.

Ask for volunteers to make illustrations of the items that were suggested, and place them on the bulletin board around the cart.

Bulletin Board Idea

The Cart: Cover the bulletin board with plain background paper. Make a large paper replica of the cart that appears in the cover illustration of the book, and put it on the bulletin board.

Introduce the Story

Show the children the illustration on the cover of the book. Ask if there is a volunteer who would like to read the title of the book to the group. Discuss the setting, the period, and the details that the illustrator has told about through this picture. Make a list of everything that can be "discovered" about the story just by looking at the illustration.

Make a prediction as to what the story will be about. Record the prediction, so that it may be read again at the finish of the story.

Procedure

If it is to be read to the group, it is suggested that this story be read in its entirety, and that you stop at some time during the reading to make some predictions. If it is to be read by the children, you may wish to utilize the DRTA Procedure, Directed Reading Thinking Activity, reading this book in sections. The Discussion Questions and Activities are given for the DRTA Procedure. If you choose to read the story in its entirety, please read over the Discussion Questions and Activities, and make choices from them. (See pages 12-15 of this guide.)

For the vocabulary words, you may wish to have the children show knowledge of some of the words. Before reading, have the children guess what the words mean. Record that simple definition. After reading, verify the meaning of each word with the children.

Using Predictions in the Novel Unit Approach

We all make predictions as we read—little guesses about what will happen next, how a conflict will be resolved, which details will be important to the plot, which details will help fill in our sense of a character. Students should be encouraged to predict, to make sensible guesses as they read the novel.

As students work on their predictions, these discussion questions can be used to guide them: What are some of the ways to predict? What is the process of a sophisticated reader's thinking and predicting? What clues does an author give to help us make predictions? Why are some predictions more likely to be accurate than others?

Create a chart for recording predictions. This could be either an individual or class activity. As each subsequent chapter is discussed, students can review and correct their previous predictions about plot and characters as necessary.

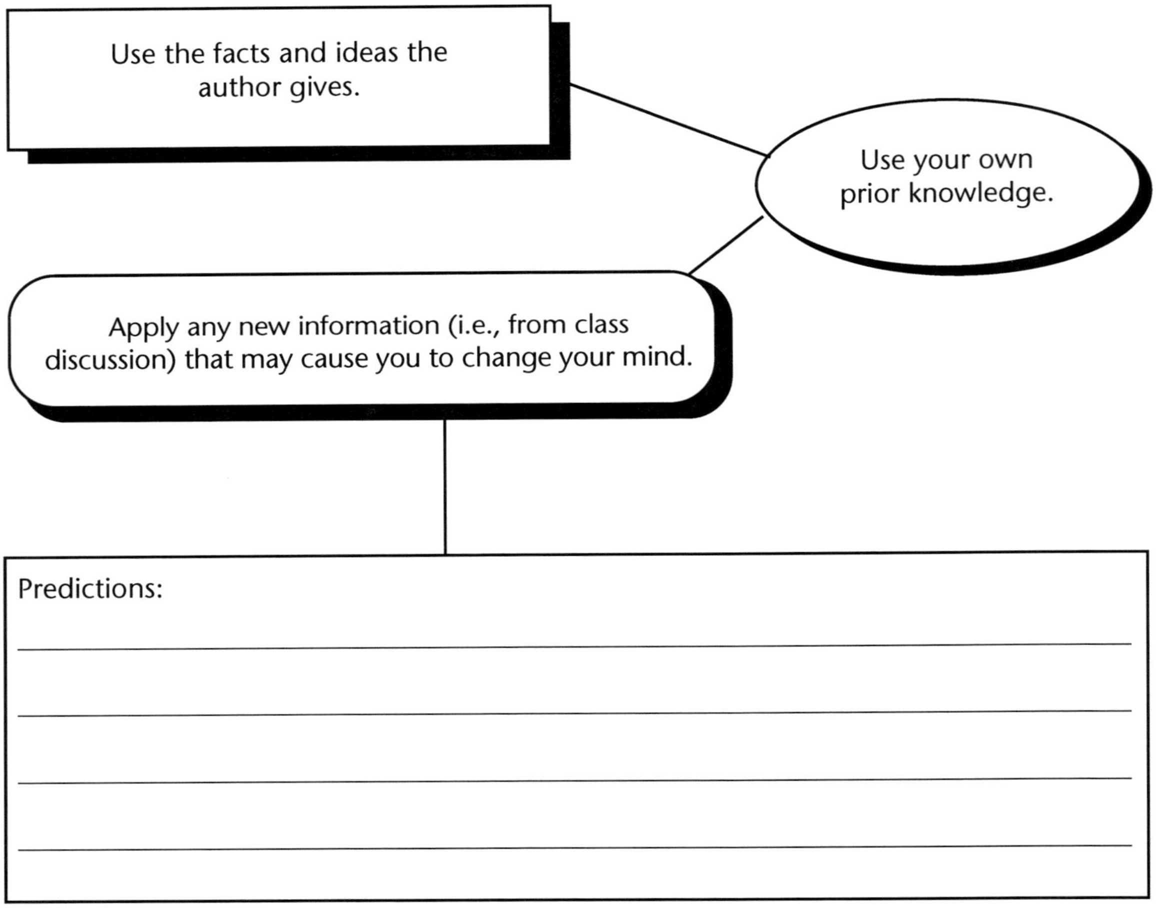

Use the facts and ideas the author gives.

Use your own prior knowledge.

Apply any new information (i.e., from class discussion) that may cause you to change your mind.

Predictions:

____

____

____

____

Prediction Chart

What characters have we met so far?	What is the conflict in the story?	What are your predictions?	Why did you make those predictions?

Setting

Problem

Goal

Episodes

Resolution

Story Map

Characters ____________________

____

Time and Place ____________________

____

Problem ____________________

____

____

Goal ____________________

____

____

Beginning ⟶ Development ⟶ Outcome

____

____

____

____

Resolution ____________________

____

____

____

Using Character Webs in the Novel Unit Approach

Attribute webs are simply a visual representation of a character from the novel. They provide a systematic way for students to organize and recap the information they have about a particular character. Attribute webs may be used after reading the novel to recapitulate information about a particular character, or completed gradually as information unfolds. They may be completed individually or as a group project.

One type of character attribute web uses these divisions:

- How a character acts and feels. (How does the character act? How do you think the character feels? How would you feel if this happened to you?)
- How a character looks. (Close your eyes and picture the character. Describe him/her to me.)
- Where a character lives. (Where and when does the character live?)
- How others feel about the character. (How does another specific character feel about our character?)

In group discussion about the characters described in student attribute webs, the teacher can ask for backup proof from the novel. Inferential thinking can be included in the discussion.

Attribute webs need not be confined to characters. They may also be used to organize information about a concept, object, or place.

Attribute Web

The attribute web below will help you gather clues the author provides about a character in the novel. Fill in the blanks with words and phrases which tell how the character acts and looks, as well as what the character says and what others say about him or her.

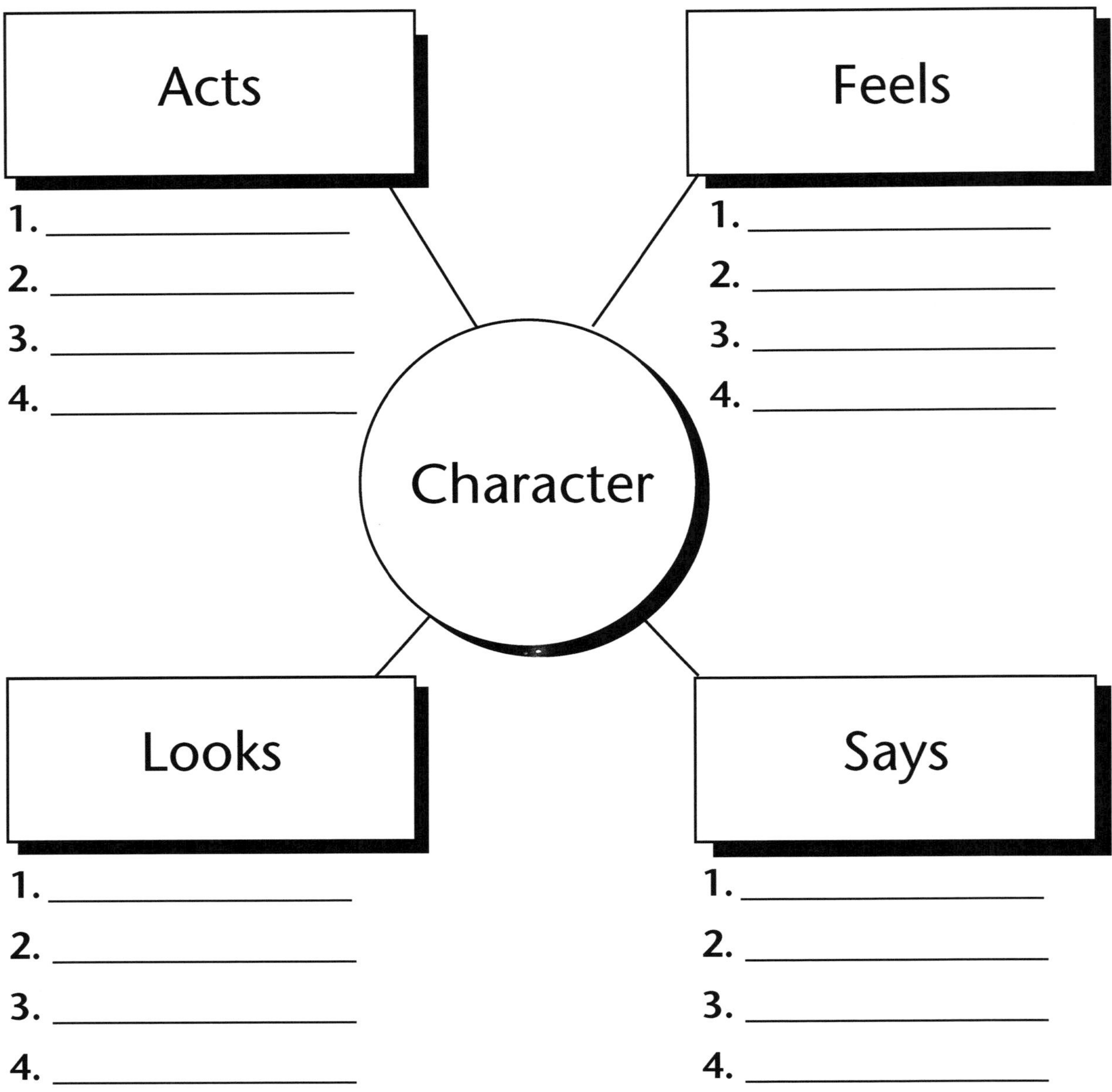

Attribute Web

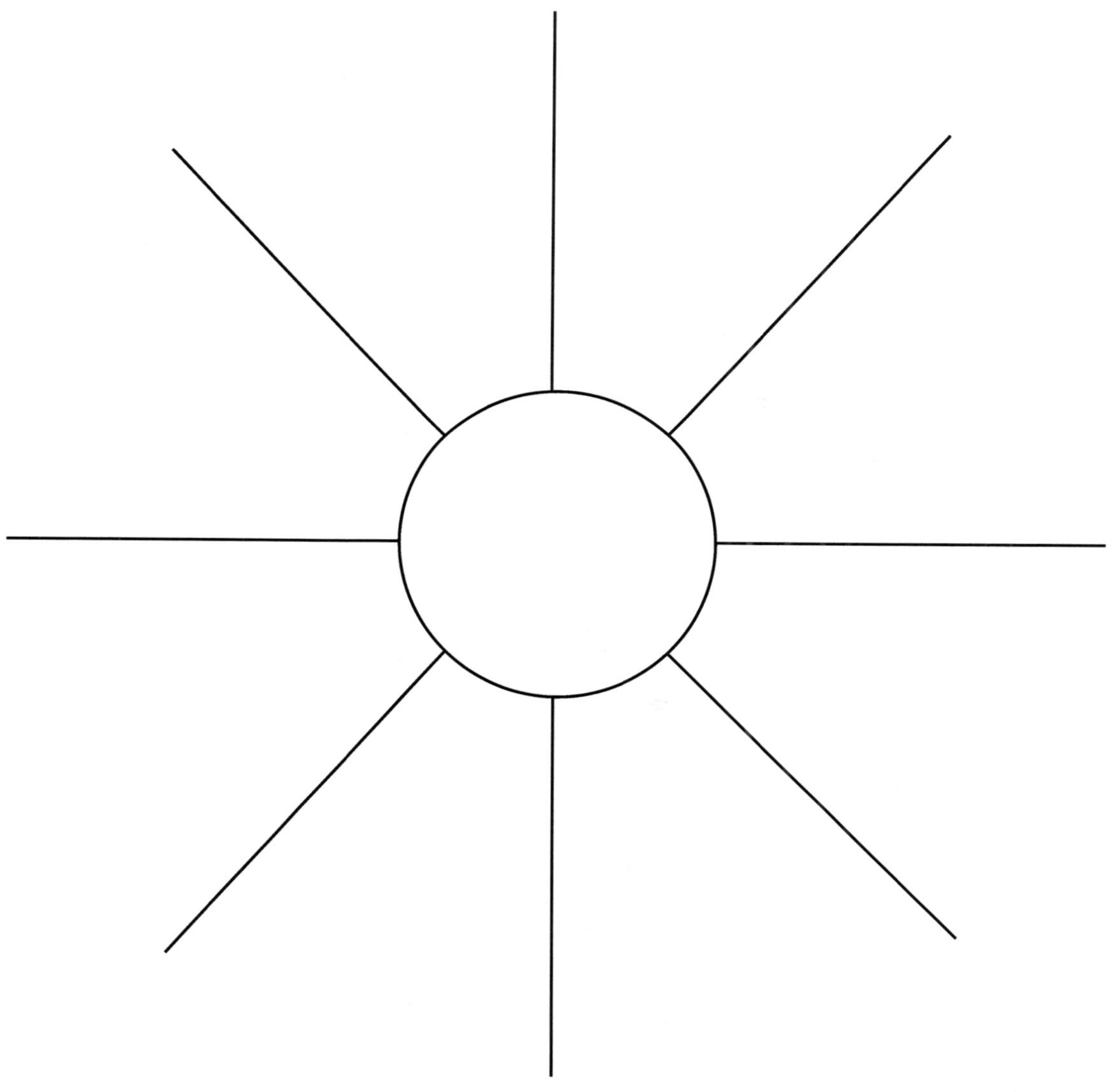

The pages of the book are unnumbered. Numbers have been assigned to the pages, starting with the illustration of the man with the ox as page 1.

Section One: Pages 1-12, From "In October..." to "...Portsmouth Market."

Vocabulary

ox (2)	cart (2)	sheared (3)
shawl (3)	spun (3)	linen (5)
flax (5)	shingles (5)	barrel (7)
honeycombs (7)	tapped (7)	villages (10)

Vocabulary Activity

Put the words in alphabetical order. Use each one in a sentence. Choose three of the words to use in the same sentence. For example: The man hitched the ox to the cart, and walked through many villages.

Discussion Questions and Activities

1. The illustrator has given clues as to the season of the year in which this story begins. Tell some of the clues, and name the season. *(Page 1, Colored leaves falling from the trees, as well as some bare branches—fall/autumn season of the year.)*
2. The author has named the month in which the story begins. What is it? *(page 2, October)*
3. What is the man packing in the cart? *(Pages 2-7, He is packing everything the family made or grew all year long that is left over. Included are: a bag of wool, a shawl, five pairs of mittens, candles, linen, shingles, birch brooms, potatoes, apples, honey, honeycombs, turnips, cabbages, maple sugar, and a bag of goose feathers.)* List the things that are packed into the cart as they are mentioned, so that there is no duplication, and so that they may be checked off as they are sold later by the man.
4. How many days does it take the man to walk to the market? *(Page 9, It takes him 10 days.)* Where is the market located? *(Page 12, The market is located in Portsmouth.)* Locate Portsmouth, New Hampshire on the map below.

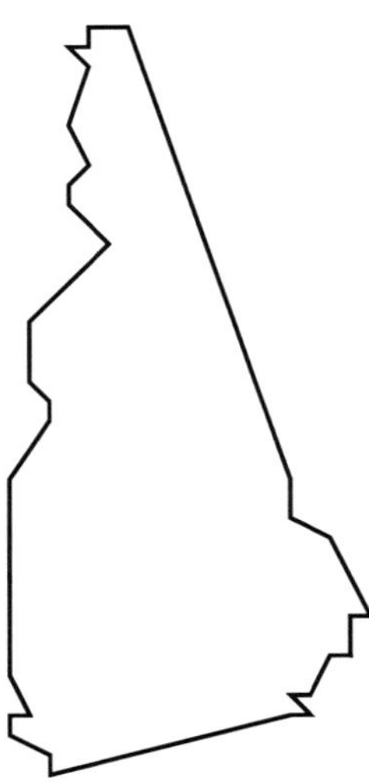

Post-reading Activities

1. Bring in some maple sugar for the children to taste.
2. Make pancakes and butter to put on the pancakes. Top with real maple syrup, and enjoy.

Buckwheat Pancakes

2 cups buckwheat flour	½ teaspoon baking soda
1 teaspoon baking powder	2½ cups milk
¾ teaspoon salt	¼ cup cooking oil or melted shortening

Combine the first four ingredients in a bowl; mix well. Add milk and oil or melted shortening; stir until smooth. Stir batter down before using each time. For each pancake, pour about ¼ cup batter onto hot, lightly greased griddle. Bake until top is covered with bubbles and edges look cooked. Turn and brown second side. Makes about 16 cakes, 4 inches in diameter.

Buttermilk Pancakes

2 cups flour	½ cup liquid shortening
2 eggs	1 teaspoon sugar
2½ cups buttermilk	1 teaspoon salt
1 teaspoon baking soda	

Sift all dry ingredients together. Beat the eggs well. Add milk and shortening. Mix well. Add liquid ingredients to dry ingredients. Heat griddle over high heat, 375° F if using automatic griddle. Drop batter onto griddle by tablespoons. Cook until bubbles appear. Turn and cook until other side is brown. Serve with butter and syrup. Makes 30 silver dollar-sized pancakes.

Butter

Whipping cream	Salt	Baby food jars

Put 1 tablespoon whipping cream into a baby food jar for each child. Cover tightly. Shake until butter forms. Pour off liquid into bowl. Add pinch of salt. Mix with a craft stick. Spread on pancake, using the craft stick as a spreader. Top with syrup. Enjoy!

3. Have samples of different kinds of materials for the children to compare the texture, weight, crushability, etc. Be sure to include a linen sample, and an all wool sample.
4. Visit the closest Historical Society in the area. Pay particular attention to the items illustrated and/or mentioned in the story.
5. Read *From Sheep to Scarf* to the children. (See Bibliography, Mitgutsch.)
6. Start a story map. (See page 8 of this guide.)
7. Start an attribute web for the man. (See pages 9-11 of this guide.)
8. Make a prediction. Do you think that the man will sell everything that he has taken to the market?

Section Two: Pages 13-20, From "He sold the bag of wool." through "...wintergreen peppermint candies."

Vocabulary

yoke (20) harness (20) wintergreen (20)

Vocabulary Activity

How many words can be made by the children from the letters in the word wintergreen? Make a list, and put it on display. Add to it as additional words are thought of as time goes by. *(Here are some: winter, green, rent, went, gent, in, win, tin, grin, wit, it, grit, tern, twig, wig, rig.)*

Discussion Questions and Activities

1. What does the man sell? *(Pages 13-20, Check off the things from the list made previously. Add to the list the wooden box, the barrel, the bag, the cart, the ox, the yoke, and harness.)* Is there anything that the author forgot to mention that was packed, but not mentioned as being sold? *(the linen)* What must we assume?
2. What does the man buy for his daughter? *(Page 20, He buys his daughter an embroidery needle.)*
3. What does the man purchase for his son? *(Page 20, He purchases a Barlow knife, for carving birch brooms.)*
4. What does the man purchase for the whole family? *(Page 20, He buys two pounds of wintergreen peppermint candies, and a kettle to hang over the fire.)*

Post-reading Activities

1. Bring in an embroidery needle and a Barlow knife, if possible, for the children to see.
2. Teach those wishing to learn how to embroider. You may wish to search out older volunteers from the local senior citizen center to help the children with this project.
3. Bring in some wintergreen peppermint candies for the children to taste. Why do you think that this would be such a special treat to the family?

Section Three: Pages 21-37, From "Then he walked home," through "...dropping feathers as soft as clouds."

Vocabulary

tucked (21) stitching (25) whittling (25)
planks (28) squawked (37)

Vocabulary Activity

Do the word search puzzle. (See Supplementary Activities.) Some additional things to do with the word search words:

1. Put the words in alphabetical order.
2. Define three of the words.
3. Use three of the words, not previously defined, in sentences. Illustrate one of the sentences.
4. Use as many of the words as you can in an original story.

Discussion Questions and Activities

1. Describe how the man carries his purchases home. *(Pages 21-22, The needle, knife, and candy are in the kettle. A stick is over his shoulder, and stuck through the kettle's handle.)* Can you think of a different way for the man to carry his purchases?
2. How do you think that the wife, son, and daughter feel about the purchases that the man has made? *(Opinion—answers will vary.)* Has anyone ever purchased something for you when away on a trip? What was it? What did you do with it?
3. On page 26, there is an illustration of the family gathered by the fire, and the author tells us that dinner is being cooked in the new kettle. What do you think might be in the kettle? What might be used today, rather than a kettle, to make a one-pot meal? *(slow cooker or electric frying pan)*

Easy Stew

2 pounds ground turkey or beef
1 onion, diced (optional)
6 potatoes, diced
6 carrots, diced
1 can green beans
1 can whole-kernel corn
1 15-ounce can tomato sauce
4 cups water
1 teaspoon salt
½ teaspoon pepper
Dash of oregano

Brown ground turkey or beef and onions; drain. Add remaining ingredients. Cook on medium heat for 20 minutes and simmer for 30 additional minutes.

4. What does the family do during the time that the snow covers the ground? *(Pages 28-31, The man gets things ready for the new ox and cart, and splits shingles. His wife makes flax into linen, his daughter embroiders linen, his son carves brooms, and everybody makes candles. In March, they tap the sugar maple trees and boil down the sap.)*
5. What do they do in April? *(Page 33, They shear the sheep, spin yarn, weave, and knit.)*
6. What do they do in May? *(Page 35, They plant potatoes, turnips, and cabbages.)*
7. Do you think that you would have liked living during the time that this story takes place? Why? Why not? (See Post-reading Activity #1.)

Post-reading Activities

1. Life was very different for the children at the time this story takes place. If you had to live as they did, what is one thing that you would really miss if you could not do it, or did not have it? Make an illustration, and write a caption to go with it.
2. Think of all of the different things that were done on the farm by the family. What would you like to do with them? Why? Write a story, and tell about what you would do on the farm with the family. Make an illustration to go with your story.
3. Bake something to share with others. Use one of the recipes given, bring in one of your own, or ask that some be shared from home.

Honey-Oatmeal Muffins

⅔ cup milk
⅓ cup vegetable oil
1 egg, beaten
¼ cup honey
1½ cups oatmeal, quick or old fashioned, uncooked
½ cup raisins
½ cup chopped nuts
⅓ cup firmly packed brown sugar
1 tablespoon baking powder
¾ teaspoon salt
1 cup all-purpose flour

Add milk, oil, egg and honey to combined remaining ingredients, mixing just until dry ingredients are moistened. Fill 12 greased or paper-lined medium-sized muffin cups ⅔ full. Bake in preheated hot oven, 400° F, 15 to 18 minutes or until golden brown. Makes one dozen muffins.

Scottish Oat Scones

⅔ cup butter or margarine, melted
⅓ cup milk
1 egg
1½ cups all-purpose flour
1¼ cups quick oatmeal, uncooked
¼ cup sugar
1 tablespoon baking powder
1 teaspoon cream of tartar
½ teaspoon salt
½ cup raisins or currants

Add butter, milk and egg to combined dry ingredients; mix just until dry ingredients are moistened. Stir in raisins. Shape dough to form ball; pat out on lightly floured surface to form an 8-inch circle. Cut into 8 to 12 wedges; bake on greased cookie sheet in preheated hot oven, 425° F, 12 to 15 minutes or until light golden brown. Serve warm with butter, preserves, or honey, as desired. Makes 8 to 12 scones.

Oatmeal Cookies

1 cup butter or margarine
1¼ cups firmly packed brown sugar
2 eggs
½ teaspoon vanilla
1¼ cups all-purpose flour
1 teaspoon soda
½ teaspoon salt
½ teaspoon cinnamon
3 cups oatmeal, quick or old fashioned, uncooked

Beat together butter and sugar until light and fluffy; blend in eggs and vanilla. Add combined flour, soda, salt, and cinnamon; mix well. Stir in oats. Drop by rounded teaspoonfuls onto greased cookie sheet; bake in preheated moderate oven, 350° F, 10 to 12 minutes or until light golden brown. Makes about 5½ dozen cookies. For variety, try adding one of the following:

1 cup raisins, 1 cup chopped nuts, 1 cup shredded or flaked coconut,
½ cup sunflower seeds, 1 cup semi-sweet chocolate flavored pieces,
1 cup butterscotch flavored pieces, 1 cup peanut butter flavored pieces,
½ cup chopped dried apricots, dates, candied fruit or cherries

4. Read *From Seed to Pear* to the children. (See Bibliography, Mitgutsch.) Ask the children to save the seeds from fruit eaten. Plant some of the seeds. Assign the care of the seeds/plants to the children. Make a record of the date(s) that the seeds are planted, and record any subsequent growth.
5. How does this story make you feel about the man and his family? What do you think might happen next in their lives? Write a new episode that tells of something different in their lives.

Supplementary Activities

1. **The Mitten Game:** You will need several pairs of mittens for this game. You may wish to borrow some from your school's lost and found, as well as use the mittens worn by the children in the group. Place the mittens in a large container, and mix them up.

   With children seated in a circle, play music and pass a mitten around the circle. When the music stops, the child holding the mitten gets to put it on. Begin passing another mitten around the circle, preferably one that is visibly different from the previous one, and start the music again. When the music stops, the child holding this mitten gets to put it on. Play continues until someone ends up wearing two matched mittens. (If the activity goes on for too long a time, you may wish to end it when a child is wearing two mittens, matched or not.)
2. **The Cart Game**: The object of the game is to be the last person to be able to recite a complete list of items, in the proper order, that will be put into the cart. Variation: This may be played as a cooperative activity, with children helping one another if something is not recalled by a player.

   Play begins by one person saying "I'm going to pack the cart, and in it I will put ___________." The first player fills in the blank with an item that begins with the letter a, such as apples. The second player must recite this sentence in its entirety and add an item that begins with the next letter of the alphabet, in this case b. For example: "I'm going to pack the cart, and in it I will put apples and blankets."

   Each of the following turns requires that the complete string of items be repeated and a new item that begins with the next letter of the alphabet be added to that string.
3. **Poetry:** Read some poems about everyday things and/or activities to the children. Discuss the content of the poems, and how it relates to their lives at this time. (See Bibliography for examples, Greenfield, de Regniers, Steig, Livingston, Janeczko.) Create a class poem.

   Read some poems about the seasons to the children. (See Bibliography, Livingston-Circle and Prelutsky-Random.) Relate the poems to the seasonal activities of the family on the farm, and to their own activities during the different seasons. Create a class poem for the current season.
4. **Man:** How many words can you think of that rhyme with the word man? Make a list. *(Here are some: ban, can, Dan, fan, Jan, Nan, pan, ran, Stan, plan, bran, clan, flan.)*

   Think of as many words as you can that begin with the same letter/sound as man. Make a list. Using words from the list, make up tongue twisters. Start with a short tongue twister at first, and try to say it fast three times. When good at it, add on to the tongue twister, to make it longer. For example:

   Mountainous Miles
   Meandering Mountainous Miles
   Miserable Meandering Mountainous Miles
   Many Miserable Meandering Mountainous Miles
5. **Consider a Product:** The man and his family made or grew most of what they needed on their farm. They sold the extras to get money to purchase the things that they were not able to manufacture themselves, such as the needle and the knife. Think about the products of today, and the process that they must go through to get to the consumer. What about a pair of mittens? a shawl? Trace a familiar product from the raw materials needed to the product

itself. How have things changed from the time of the Ox-Cart man? (See Bibliography, Mitgutsch.)

6. **For Sale:** The way in which consumers get the goods they need has changed a great deal since the time of this story. However, products may still be sold to get money to enable people to accomplish a goal.

   Set a goal, for the purchase of something, such as a portion of a rain forest, the conservation of the wetlands, etc. Plan, and have, a bake sale, "garage sale," used toy sale, or something similar. Allow the children to earn the money that they will use to obtain the established goal. They will need to obtain the product(s) to be sold, advertise, price merchandise, and carry out the actual sale. They will then have to determine if they have enough money to accomplish the goal that they have set.

   Some money activities to try before sending it off:

   a) Sort the money by kind, putting all of the pennies together, etc.
   b) Count the pennies. Put them into sets of ten as they are counted. Record the total value of the pennies.
   c) Line up the nickels for ease of counting. Skip count by fives as the nickels are counted. Depending upon the abilities of the children doing the activity, you may wish to have the nickels placed in rows of one hundred as they are counted. How many nickels are in each row of one hundred? Record the total value of the nickels.
   d) Line up the dimes. Skip count by tens. Place the dimes in rows, each with a total value of one hundred. How many dimes are in a row that has a total value of one hundred? Record the total value of the dimes.
   e) Look at the quarters. How many quarters are needed to have the value of 100 cents, or $1.00? Place the quarters in stacks of four, each representing one dollar/100 cents. Record the total value of the quarters.
   f) Look at the fifty-cent pieces. How many fifty-cent pieces are needed to have the value of 100 cents, or $1.00? Place the fifty-cent pieces in stacks of two, each representing one dollar/100 cents. Record the total value of the fifty-cent pieces.
   g) Look at the dollar bills. There is a picture of the head of a person on one side of the bill. Who is that person? *(George Washington)* Can you tell us something about that person? Why do you think that his picture is on the dollar bill? Count the dollar bills. How many do you have? How many cents are represented by these dollar bills? How many nickels? How many dimes? How many quarters? How many fifty-cent pieces?
   h) What is the total amount of money earned? Compare the total to the amount needed for the chosen project. Do you have enough?

   You may wish to contact one or more of the following agencies for information:

   National Wildlife Federation
   1400 Sixteenth Street, NW
   Washington, DC 20036-2266

   Rainforest Alliance
   270 Lafayette St., Suite 512
   New York, NY l0012

   Rainforest Action Network
   450 Sansome, Suite 700
   San Francisco, CA 94111

   National Institute for Urban Wildlife
   10921 Trotting Ridge Way
   Columbia, MD 21044

7. **Cows in the Meadow:** The man has decided to purchase some cows for the farm. He goes to a sale, and is given some information about the brown and black cows that are on sale. The man is told that four black cows and three brown cows give as much milk in five days as three black cows and four brown cows give in four days. What color cows would you advise the man to purchase in order to get the most milk to sell? *(brown)*
8. **Creative Clothing:** For this activity you will need light weight paper, such as poster paper, newsprint, or something similar cut into 6 or 9 inch squares, scissors, glue and/or stapler with additional staples.

   Two of the squares of paper are used at a time, one placed on top of the other so that it appears that only one piece of paper is being used. These are held together, and folded in half. A child then draws one-half of the article of clothing onto the fold of the paper. (Please see illustration.) Paper remains folded as the one-half of the item of clothing is cut out. The piece of clothing is then unfolded to produce the complete garment. The two pieces of the garment are then glued or stapled together to make the item of clothing. Finishing touches may then be added.

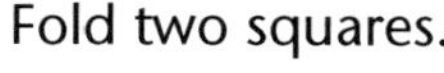

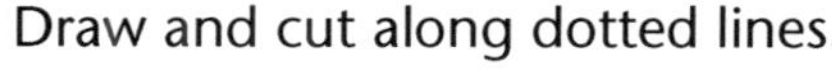

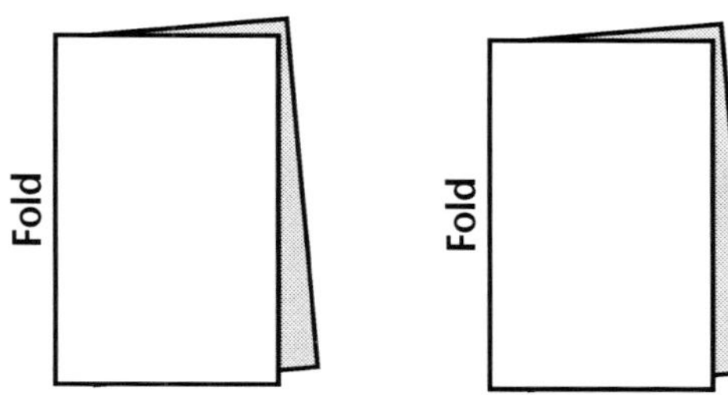

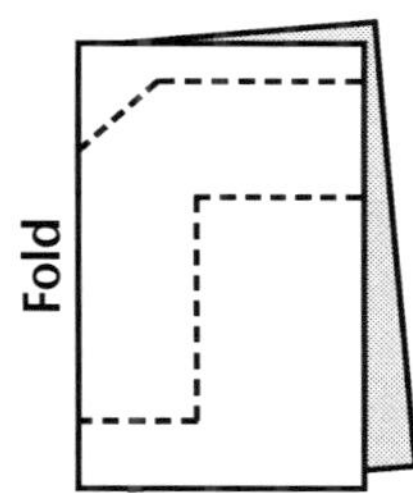

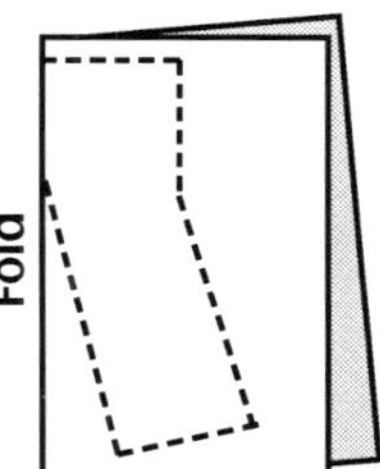

Unfold and "seam" with glue or staples.

9. **A Birthday Candle:** At the time that this story takes place, the family used candles to provide the light needed for early morning and evening activities. Just how long might a candle give off light?

   For this activity you will need a birthday candle placed in a lump of plasticine, so that it will stand up, matches, a stop watch or clock with a second hand, a piece of paper and a crayon or pencil for each child.

   The object of the activity is to estimate the length of time that the candle will burn, and then to find out by timing the actual burning of the candle.

Give each child a piece of paper and a crayon or pencil. Ask that each estimate the length of time that the candle will burn, and to record that on the paper. Fold the paper, so that the estimation is "private."

Light the candle, and record the time. As the candle burns, ask if the time has been reached that has been recorded on the paper. (It will usually turn out that the estimated times are much too short, and that recorded times will be reached quickly.) After the candle goes out, discuss the findings. What conclusions may be drawn?

Teacher Information/Burning Candle:

a) The heat from the flame of the match melts the wax on the wick. This wax evaporates.
b) The temperature of the flame ignites the wax vapor, which begins to burn.
c) The heat from the burning wax vapor melts more wax at the base of the wick.
d) This liquid wax travels up the wick by capillary action, like water up a string, where it evaporates and burns. (If some wax runs down the side of the candle, and remains unburnt as the candle is used, it does NOT represent all of the original wax, but only that portion that has not become vapor and burned.)

10. **A Balancing Act:** The children in the family did not have television, movies, videos, etc. to use in their free time. They had to use what they had on hand for entertainment. Do you think that they might have had fun trying this?

    For this activity you will need an old-fashioned gallon jug that will retain its shape, and may be sat upon, or a ball that may be sat upon, a crayon, and a 3 x 5 index card for each person doing the activity.

    Place the jug on its side on the floor or ground. The person doing the activity sits on the jug, with legs outstretched, and one heel placed on the toe of the other foot. The player is allowed to touch the floor only when obtaining balance. In one hand the player has the crayon, and in the other the card. The player tries to print his/her name on the card while balancing on the jug.

Vocabulary Word Search Puzzle

Do the word search. Write down the letters that have not been used, starting at the top, and working left to right in each row. Group the letters into words to find the hidden message.

w	i	n	t	e	r	g	r	e	e	n	t
h	i	h	o	n	e	y	c	o	m	b	s
i	a	n	h	s	h	i	n	g	l	e	s
t	s	r	t	u	c	k	e	d	b	e	p
t	t	v	n	e	o	o	x	c	a	a	u
l	i	i	r	e	r	t	x	c	r	m	n
i	t	l	t	a	s	h	e	a	r	e	d
n	c	l	a	l	q	s	n	r	e	y	w
g	h	a	p	i	u	a	h	t	l	o	l
k	i	g	p	n	a	p	l	a	n	k	s
e	n	e	e	e	w	d	h	o	w	e	m
e	g	s	d	n	k	f	l	a	x	l	x

WINTERGREEN
SQUAWK
OX
SHAWL
FLAX
BARREL
WINTER
TUCKED
LINEN
STITCHING
TAPPED
SHEARED
SHINGLES
WHITTLING
PLANKS
SPUN
HONEYCOMBS
VILLAGES
HARNESS
YOKE
CART

(Answer: THE OX CART MAN WALKED HOME.)

Legend: Second x = period (.)
[For this unit, the second "x" will become a period.]

Some additional things to do with the word search words:

1. Which of the words has the most letters? Which word has the least letters? How many more letters does the longest word have than the shortest? *(Longest: wintergreen/11 letters; Shortest: ox/2 letters; Wintergreen has 9 more letters than ox.)*
2. Choose six of the words to make a graph to show how many letters are in each of the words. Compare the number of letters in each. Make some concluding statements. For example: Telling which word has the most letters, which word has the least, and if any are equal.
3. How many words can you make from the letters in *honeycombs* in five minutes? *(Here are some: honey, comb, yen, mob, bone, hone, some, son, ...)*

Crossword Puzzle

Across

3. Thin sheet of wood
4. Thick board
6. Holds honey
10. Plant

Down

1. Cloth made of flax
2. A community
5. Wooden frame
7. Two-wheeled vehicle
8. Wooden container
9. A bull

Use as many of the words from the puzzle as you can to write a story of your own, or to write a report about the *Ox-Cart Man.*

(Words used: barrel, cart, flax, honeycomb, linen, ox, plank, shingle, village, yoke.)

Teacher Information

Ox

Oxen include domestic cattle, water buffalo, bison, musk oxen, brahman, yak, banteng, and other members of the bovine family. Most oxen first came from Asia and Europe. The musk ox and bison are natives of North America. South America, Australia, and Madagascar have no native oxen.

Oxen have heavy bodies, long tails, divided hoofs, and they chew their cud. Their horns are smooth, curved, and stand out from the sides of their heads. Domestic oxen supply meat, milk, and leather. They are powerful work animals and serve as beasts of burden in some parts of the world. (Source: *World Book Encyclopedia*, 1991.)

The Cart

From the earliest of times, man has civilized himself by finding ways to do things more easily and efficiently. Cattle were tamed, and then the ox was used to carry the load usually carried by man. Man then found out that the ox could drag more than he could carry, so a carrier for the goods was developed. In time, heavy loads were moved on rollers, the rollers being placed on the ground ahead of the load, then moved from behind after the load, on a sledge, had passed over them.

Eventually, light loads moved by oxen also utilized rollers for easier movement. The rollers then became wheels, and the sledge a cart. Tree-trunk wheels were used by the Romans on farm carts. They were called tympani, because they were shaped like drums. These simple drum-wheels split easily because of the wood grain. Solid wheels, made of thick planks pinned together came next. The grain of these wheels ran at a right angle to the axle.

Before recorded history, someone made a wheel with a hub, spokes, and fellies. *(Felly: One section of the rim of a wheel.)* This wheel was lighter and stronger than that of previous times. The first carts were used for hauling. Their use as a means of passenger movement came later. The cart used by the *Ox-Cart Man* resembles the Red River cart of the 1860s. This cart was made entirely of hand-hewn wood, the hubs and wheel fellies lashed together with rawhide.

Portsmouth, New Hampshire

Portsmouth is the chief seaport on the coast of New Hampshire. The city is a commercial center of southeastern New Hampshire. Portsmouth was founded as Strawbery Banke in 1630, and was incorporated as a city in 1849. The city lies at the mouth of the Piscataqua River. At present, the Portsmouth Naval Shipyard and Pease Air Force Base are nearby. The city has a number of corporate offices and financial institutions. Its attractions include Strawbery Banke, a restored historic area and many houses that date from the 1700s or early 1800s. (Source: *World Book Encyclopedia*, 1991.)

Bibliography

Beall, Pamela Conn and Susan Hagen Nipp. *Wee Sing Sing-alongs.* Los Angeles, CA: Price/Stern/Sloan, 1990. Page 20, "She'll Be Comin' Round the Mountain"

de Regniers, Beatrice. *Poems Children Will Sit Still For.* NY: Scholastic, 1969. Page 18, "Our Tree"; Page 22, "Weather"; Page 27, "Galoshes"

Greenfield, Eloise. *Under The Sunday Tree.* NY: Harper and Row, 1988. Page 2, "To Catch a Fish"; Page 16, "The Tree"; Page 32, "Under The Sunday Tree"; Page 36, "Buddies"

Janeczko, Paul, Selected by. *This Delicious Day.* NY: Orchard Books/Watts, 1987. Page 3, "In The Morning"; Page 7, "The Crow"; Page 10, "The Loaves"; Page 34, "Gone"

Livingston, Myra. *Remembering and Other Poems.* NY: Margaret K. McElderry Books, 1989. Page 1, "Apple Tree"; Page 13, "Ladybug"; Page 14, "Leaf Boats"

Livingston, Myra. *A Circle of Seasons.* NY: Holiday House, 1982.

Mitgutsch. Ali. *From Grain to Bread.* Minneapolis, MN: Carolrhoda Books, 1981.

Mitgutsch, Ali. *From Beet to Sugar.* Minneapolis, MN: Carolrhoda Books, 1981.

Mitgutsch, Ali. *From Sheep to Scarf.* Minneapolis, MN: Carolrhoda Books, 1981.

Mitgutsch, Ali. *From Sand to Glass.* Minneapolis, MN: Carolrhoda Books, 1981.

Mitgutsch, Ali. *From Cotton to Pants.* Minneapolis, MN: Carolrhoda Books, 1981.

Mitgutsch, Ali. *From Blossom to Honey.* Minneapolis, MN: Carolrhoda Books, 1981.

Mitgutsch, Ali. *From Cow to Shoe.* Minneapolis, MN: Carolrhoda Books, 1981.

Mitgutsch, Ali. *From Milk to Ice Cream.* Minneapolis, MN: Carolrhoda Books, 1981.

Mitgutsch, Ali. *From Cacao Bean to Chocolate.* Minneapolis, MN: Carolrhoda Books, 1981.

Mitgutsch, Ali. *From Fruit to Jam.* Minneapolis, MN: Carolrhoda Books, 1981.

Mitgutsch, Ali. *From Grass to Butter.* Minneapolis, MN: Carolrhoda Books, 1981.

Mitgutsch, Ali. *From Seed to Pear.* Minneapolis, MN: Carolrhoda Books, 1981.

Mitgutsch, Ali. *From Tree to Table.* Minneapolis, MN: Carolrhoda Books, 1981.

Prelutsky, Jack, compiler. *The Random House Book of Poetry for Children.* NY: Random House, 1983. (See the section "The Four Seasons.")

Steig, Jeanne. *Consider The Lemming.* NY: Sunburst/Farrar, Straus and Giroux, 1988. (Pages are unnumbered. "The Hare," "The Pig," "The Cat," "The Dog")

Tunis, Edwin. *Wheels.* NY: Thomas Y. Crowell, 1955.

Puzzle Answers

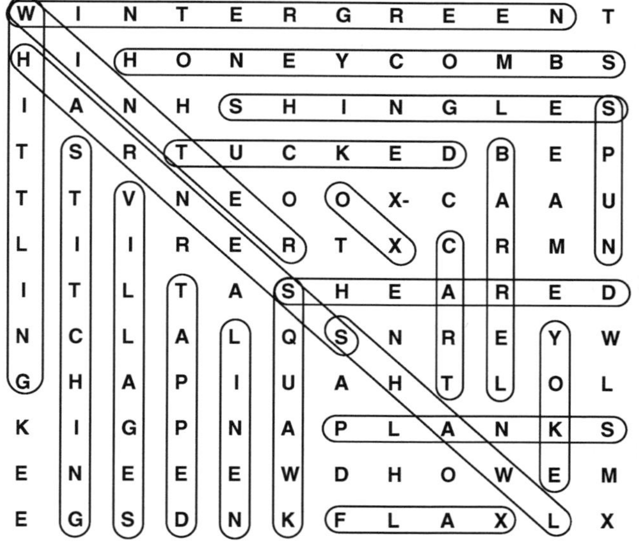

Assessment for *Ox-Cart Man*

Assessment is an on-going process. The following ten items can be completed during the novel study. Once finished, the student and teacher will check them. Points may be added to indicate the level of understanding.

Name ______________________________ Date _________________

Student	Teacher		
_______	_______	1.	Fill in predicting ideas before reading the book—either on a prediction chart (see page 6) or on a class list.
_______	_______	2.	Tell a little bit about the book's author and illustrator.
_______	_______	3.	Review the story's plot on a story map (see page 8).
_______	_______	4.	Fill in an attribute web for the Ox-Cart Man.
_______	_______	5.	Make a collage or poster of all the things the man put in his cart.
_______	_______	6.	What would *you* take to market in a cart? Answer in a drawing.
_______	_______	7.	Do the Vocabulary Word Search Puzzle on page 21.
_______	_______	8.	With a partner, do the Crossword Puzzle on page 22.
_______	_______	9.	Give yourself credit for other vocabulary activities you complete.
_______	_______	10.	Is it thumbs up or thumbs down for this book? Give reasons for your answer.

Notes

Notes